I'm Reading About

MINNESOTA

The North Star State!

GALLOPADE

by Carole Marsh

Printed and Manufactured in Peachtree City, GA., USA
www.gallopade.com

Book design: John Hanson

Editorial manager: Janice Baker

Minnesota is a great state.

It is one of a kind.

What makes Minnesota special?

Let's read about it and see!

NATIVE AMERICANS

Who lived in Minnesota first?

Native Americans did!

They moved around to find food.
They hunted in Minnesota's woods.
They fished in Minnesota's rivers.
They gathered fruits and seeds and nuts.

EXPLORERS

The first explorers came to Minnesota in the 1650s.
They came from the country of France.

These explorers were fur traders.
They were also looking for new land!

SETTLEMENT

Fort Snelling was one of the first settlements in Minnesota.
It was a military fort.
Fort Snelling was built to protect the area from the British.

Fort Snelling was named after Colonel Josiah Snelling.
He supervised the building of the fort.

Fort Snelling

STATEHOOD

Minnesota was the 32nd state
to join the United States of America!

Isn't it great,
to be a state!
I bet Minnesota
could hardly wait!

Minnesota became a state in 1858.

Minnesota

The 32nd State

FLAG

I am the state flag.
I was adopted in 1957.

What color am I?
I am blue.

Look at me.
What else do you see?

I fly high over the state of Minnesota!

1858
L'ETOILE DU NORD
1819
1893
MINNESOTA

CAPITAL

Say hello to St. Paul,
the capital city of Minnesota!

There is an important building in St. Paul.
It is the State Capitol.
Minnesota's laws are made there!

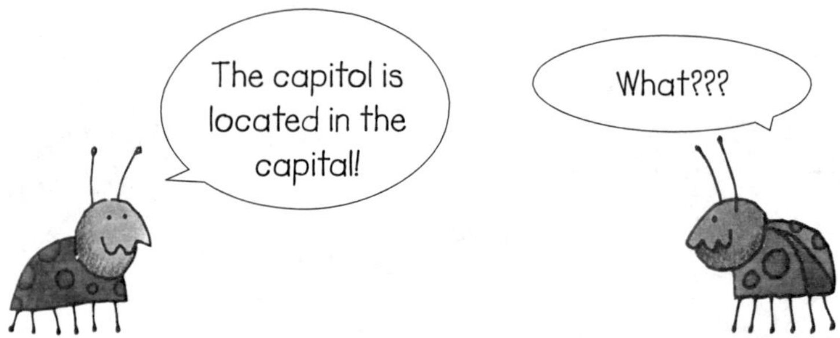

Capitol
St. Paul
Capital

SEAL

I am a seal,
but I am not the State Seal.
If I were, I would be very important.
I would be stamped on many official papers.
(Ouch, that might hurt!)

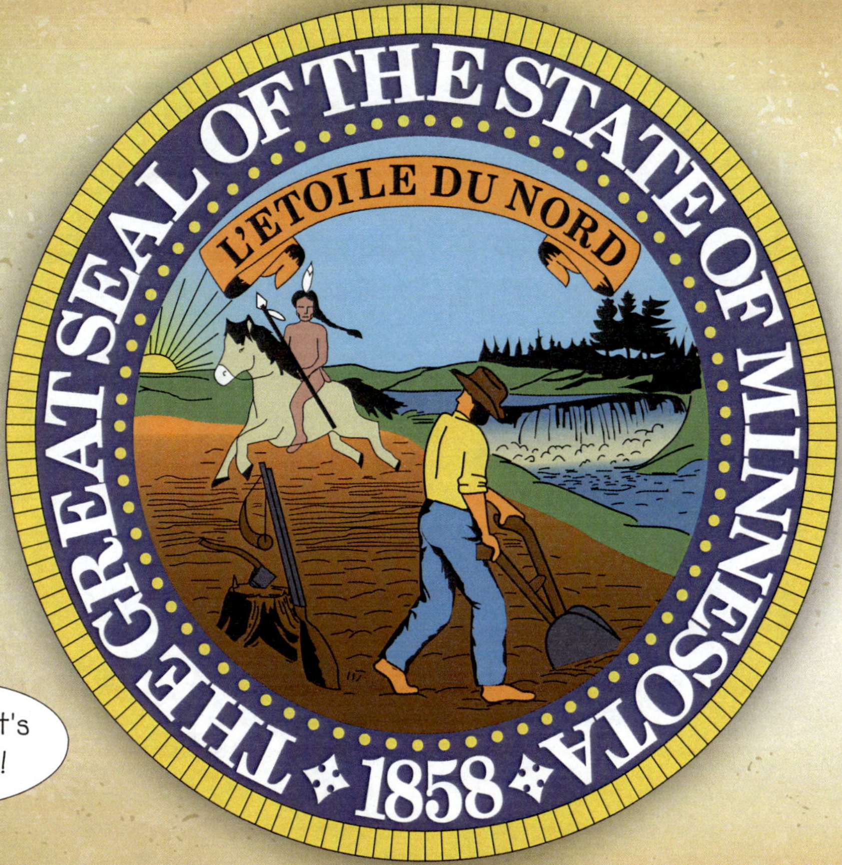
THE GREAT SEAL OF THE STATE OF MINNESOTA
L'ETOILE DU NORD
1858

Now, that's official!

NICKNAME

State nicknames are fun!
State nicknames are great!
They share fun facts
about each state!

Minnesota's nickname is "The North Star State."

Minnesota is farther north than any other state in the United States!

The North Star State

BORDERS

Look at Minnesota.
Minnesota is in a region called "the Midwest."

Minnesota borders five other states.
It also borders the country of Canada.
Find Minnesota and its neighbors on the map.

Minnesota shares a water border (Lake Superior) with Michigan.

Borders

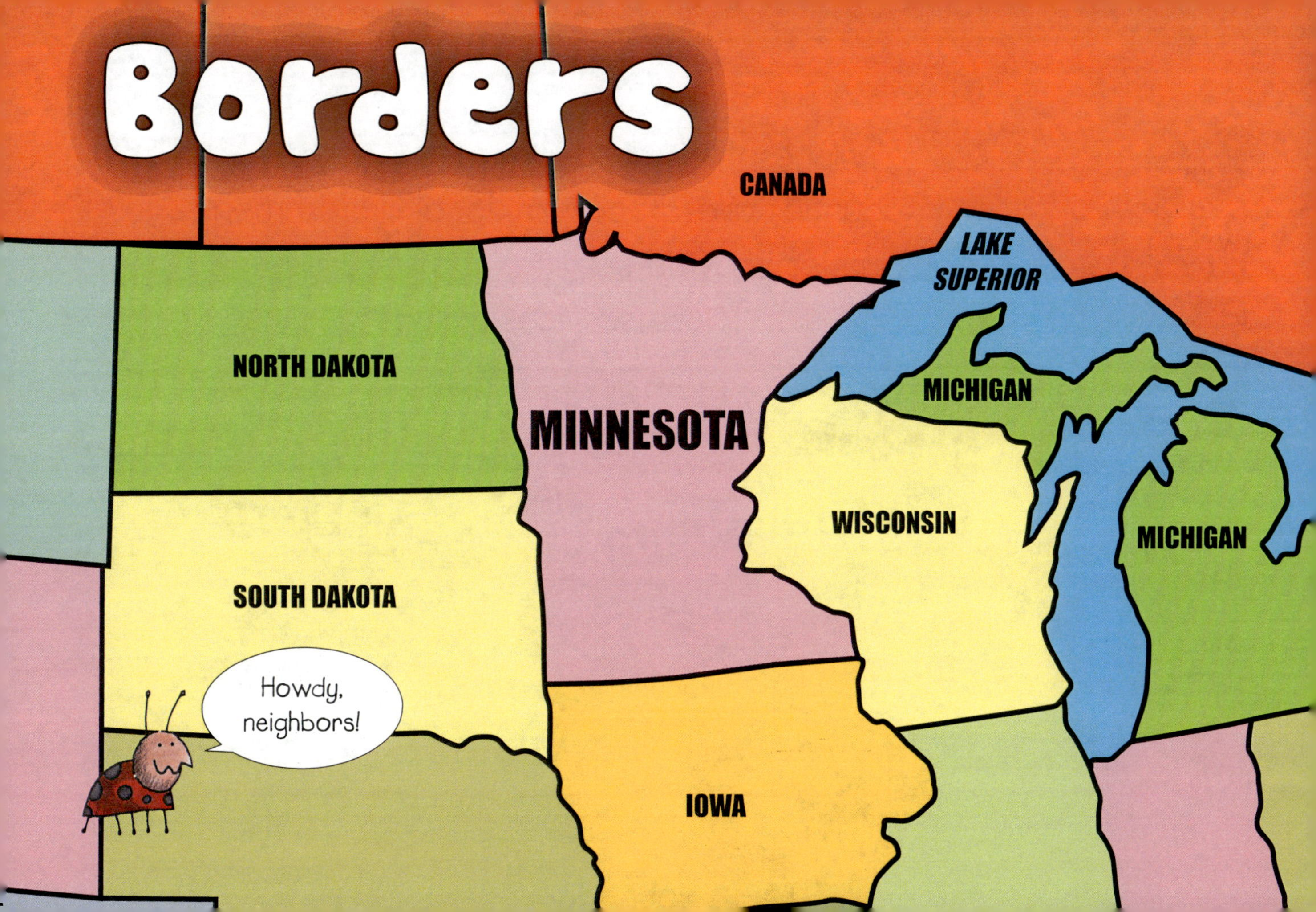
CANADA
LAKE SUPERIOR
NORTH DAKOTA
MINNESOTA
MICHIGAN
WISCONSIN
MICHIGAN
SOUTH DAKOTA
Howdy, neighbors!
IOWA

COUNTIES

Minnesota is divided into 87 counties.
Counties are a form of local government.
Counties provide services that people need!
Those services include:

Schools **Parks** **Libraries** **Police**

Firefighters **and More!**

Counties

MINNESOTA'S CAPITAL, ST. PAUL, IS IN RAMSEY COUNTY.

Many famous people

Francis Scott Fitzgerald

Novelist who wrote *The Great Gatsby*

Rose Totino

Co-founder of Totino's Frozen Pizza

Charles Schulz

Cartoonist who created the Peanuts comic strip

call our state home!

Walter Mondale
ice President of the United States under President Jimmy Carter

Arthur Fry
Co-inventor of 3M Post-It Notes

Roger Maris
Professional baseball player who broke the home run record in 1961

PEOPLE

Common Loon

I am the state bird, and I fly
over Minnesota, proud and high.

As I fly, up in the sky,
I flap my wings to tell you "Hi!"

The Minnesota state bird is the Common Loon.

BIRD

Lady's Slipper

FLOWER

I am the Lady's Slipper.
I am the state flower.

I grow where it's mild and sunny.
I bloom in spring and summer.
I help make Minnesota beautiful!

Look at me! Smell me!
I am a special type of orchid.

Norway Pine

TREE

I am a Norway Pine—I'm the state tree.
All over Minnesota is where to find me.

My roots run deep, they keep me strong.
My leaves stay green, all year long.

I stand up straight, big and tall.
Don't climb too high—it would hurt to fall!

Monarch Butterfly

I am the Monarch Butterfly.
I am the state insect.

I flit and I fly from flower to flower.
I am looking for nectar to drink.

Look at my beautiful wings.
What colors do you see?

Lake Superior

LAKES

Let's go to the lake!

We can wade in the water.
We can ride on a boat.

We can jump off the dock
onto an inner tube float!

Lake Superior, Minnesota's Great Lake,
is home to many animals:

Fish Snakes Birds Turtles Salamanders and More!

Sawtooth Mountains

MOUNTAINS

Minnesota's Sawtooth Mountains are the place to be.
Hiking, fishing, camping—
fun for you and me.

Winter weather brings lots of snow.
Temperatures drop to freezing and below!

Rivers

RIVERS

Minnesota has many rivers.
People like to use rivers for boating and fishing!

This habitat is home to many animals:

Birds **Deer** **Snakes** **Frogs** **Fish** **and More!**

Many of Minnesota's early settlers built towns along rivers.

Mall of America

LANDMARK

The Mall of America is the second largest mall in the United States! It is located in Bloomington, Minnesota. There is a theme park called Nickelodeon Universe inside the mall.

The Mall of America has more than 500 stores!

Minnesota Crops

AGRICULTURE

Minnesota has many farms.
Why?
Because Minnesota has good soil and a mild climate!

Some of the top crops grown in Minnesota are:

Corn **Soybeans** **Sugarbeets** **Green Peas**

Sports in Minnesota

SPORTS

Baseball! Basketball! Football! Hockey!
Minnesota has it all.

Whether you like to watch or play,
You are sure to have a ball!

Twins Timberwolves Vikings

Wild

Golden Gophers

Bulldogs & More!

Minnesota: Home of 10,000 Lakes

CLAIM TO FAME

Minnesota is known as the "Land of 10,000 Lakes." There are large and small lakes all over the state. Melting glaciers formed the lakes.

Actually, there may be more than 11,000 lakes in Minnesota!

GLOSSARY

climate: weather conditions in an area over a long period of time

glacier: a slowly moving mass of ice

habitat: a place where plants or animals naturally live

laws: rules made by the government

nectar: a sweet liquid produced by plants, especially flowers

region: an area that has similar characteristics

settlement: the first community in an area

supervise: to observe and direct the work of someone else